KU-371-747

An
Illustrated History of
Harrow School

An
Illustrated History of
Harrow School

Patrick Lichfield & Richard Shymansky
with Jim Golland

WILTSHIRE LIBRARY & MUSEUM SERVICE

MICHAEL JOSEPH · LONDON

MICHAEL JOSEPH LTD

Published by the Penguin Group
27 Wrights Lane, London W8 5TZ, England
Viking Penguin Inc., 40 West 23rd Street, New York, New York 10010, USA
Penguin Books Australia Ltd, Ringwood, Victoria, Australia
Penguin Books Canada Ltd, 2801 John Street, Markham, Ontario, Canada L3R 1B4
Penguin Books (NZ) Ltd, 182–190 Wairau Road, Auckland 10, New Zealand

Penguin Books Ltd. Registered Offices: Harmondsworth, Middlesex, England

First published in Great Britain 1988

Head Master's Introduction © Ian Beer, 1988
Captions and Notes on the Photographs © Jim Golland, 1988
Photographs © as ascribed on the Photographic Acknowledgements Page, 1988

All rights reserved. Without limiting the rights under copyright reserved
above, no part of this publication may be reproduced, stored
in, or introduced into a retrieval system, or transmitted, in any form
or by any means (electronic, mechanical, photocopying,
recording or otherwise), without the prior written permission of both
the copyright owner and the above publisher of this book

Made and printed in Great Britain by
Butler & Tanner Ltd, Frome, Somerset

Filmset in Palatino by KeyStar, St. Ives, Cambridge

ISBN 0 7181 3151 7

Head Master's introduction

A great number of books have been written on the independent schools of Great Britain, and many about Harrow School and its particular position in influencing education in this country and countries worldwide, but never before has anyone attempted an illustrated history, despite the photogenic quality of Harrow on the Hill, its buildings, its people and their activities. This is all the more surprising as the long-established firm of Hills & Saunders have had a studio on the Hill since 1872, and for over ten years before that Edwyn Goshawk had practised as a photographer. On his death, Hills & Saunders acquired Goshawk's studio with much of its unsold stock and props, and this continuity of business has resulted in a remarkable series of prints from the late 1850s, depicting many aspects of School life; and from the 1860s to the last war, the glass negatives from which these were taken survive virtually intact.

Hills & Saunders is now owned by Mr Richard Shymansky, one of the authors of this book.

The close links between Harrow and photography go back almost to the origins of the process; this association may well have been promoted by that dynamic and innovative Head Master, Dr C. J. Vaughan, who owned one of the earliest collections of daguerrotypes to have been assembled – unfortunately now dispersed. Vaughan's enthusiasm was infectious and his example was quickly followed by various masters who started to keep albums of portraits of their family, friends and pupils, and by house masters who inaugurated the practice of having house groups photographed and particular achievements recorded.

It is particularly appropriate, therefore, that Henry Fox Talbot the leading British pioneer of photography, who invented the negative/positive technique upon which all photography is now based, was an Old Boy of Harrow School.

A precocious, brilliant and sensitive boy, Fox Talbot had attended the School for four years from 1811. His Head Master was Dr George Butler, father of a later Master of Trinity College, Cambridge, and the Head Master clearly had to discipline this imaginative young man quite firmly whilst he was a boy within the Head Master's House at the School. A letter from Talbot's mother to the boy's aunt makes the situation very clear indeed:

> 'As he can no longer continue his experiments in Dr Butler's House, he resorts to a good natured blacksmith who lets him explode as much as he pleases. He makes "Pulvis Fulminans", and I am quite nervous at the thought of the risks he must run with Potassium Nitrate, Sulphur and Potash. He has been trying to guild steel with a solution of Nitromuriate of Gold. This was the fatal experiment which blew him up at Dr Butler's as it exploded with the noise of a pistol and attacked the olfactory nerves of the whole household. Dr Butler was alarmed and declared the Sun Fire Office would not insure his House for a single day!'

Subsequently Dr Butler stated that henceforward only the theory of Chemistry was to be studied at Harrow School! Not that this deterred our young scholar, for having moved his experiments to the blacksmith's, he encouraged his mother to continue to supply him with his chemicals. After graduating at Cambridge Fox Talbot combined scientific research with being a Member of Parliament and a county administrator for Wiltshire.

PHOTO BY RICHARD SHYMANSKY

Mr Ian Beer, Head Master

Photography became something of a popular craze by the early twentieth century, and this was as true at Harrow School as elsewhere. A Photographic Society was established in 1913, and recently, under the direction of Mr R. P. Murray, its members have been winning national photographic competitions.

The second great name in the history of photography as far as Harrow School is concerned is that of Sir Cecil (W.H.) Beaton (page 83). He was at the School from 1918 to 1922, when he left to enter Clare College, Cambridge. He became a photographic artist working as, among other things, an official photographer for the Ministry of Information in India, Burma and China during the Second World War.

The third well-known photographer to be educated at Harrow is, of course, the co-author of this volume, Patrick Lichfield, who joined Elmfield House in 1952, leaving five years later to enter the Royal Military Academy at Sandhurst. For three years he served with the Grenadier Guards, retiring his commission to begin his career as a photographer. We are indebted to him, not only for this book, but for his many photographs of Harrow Hill.

The photographs selected for this book give us a pictorial record of about 150 years of the School's history; the previous 260 years or so were before the creation of the art of photography, and for information about them the written word must suffice. We shall be indebted to Dr Christopher Tyerman when his new official history of the School is published in a few years' time, but we are sure he will be the first to acknowledge that some of the early photographs published here will assist readers in imagining the atmosphere and conditions under which boys and masters of Harrow School thrived in earlier times.

The final pages of this pictorial record give clues to the future, for the advent of the computer and the technological revolution in which we now live will inspire this generation and those that follow to participate in a very different educational world from that portrayed at the start of the book. Pupils will be taught how to adapt to change at an even faster rate than their predecessors; they will be involved in a world of information technology which will link pictures of their school almost instantaneously with those of a school in, say, Peking or Los Angeles.

It therefore becomes all the more important that pupils, parents and teachers should be able to browse through this book and realise through its pictorial impact how grateful we must be to our predecessors, and for the wonderful heritage entrusted to us at this time in a long school history.

Ian Beer.

Ian Beer
1988

A portrait of Henry Fox Talbot taken by Moffatt Studio of Edinburgh 1864.

Photo: Fox Talbot Museum Collection

A note on the photographs

A few years ago, Hills & Saunders, the School photographers, changed hands, and my attention was drawn to their stock of glass negatives. Enquiries were made, and eventually, the entire collection was temporarily transferred to the School premises to enable an assessment to be made of its potential value as an archival record. Mr R. P. Murray, the master in charge of the School Photographic Society, very kindly allowed us to use his newly converted studio to store the negatives in more suitable conditions than the rather damp basements and garden sheds that had been their home previously.

Vast numbers of boxes started to arrive, and we became a little overwhelmed at the magnitude of the task we had set ourselves: at the last count, there were well over 50,000 negatives. The more interesting seemed to be on plates 10"×12": these were usually boxed in eights and had been carefully numbered and identified; record books assisted the process of recording them. Many, however, were loose and none were in any order. Some of the boxes had been damaged and had been attacked by damp. The negatives themselves were often corroded, cracked or stained, with emulsion peeling off. None of the recognised methods of archival storage had been applied and remedial work was obviously going to be needed. We had heard, too, alarming stories of earlier misadventures: one previous owner had apparently gladdened the hearts of local gardeners by letting them have these large glass plates for glazing greenhouses – once the annoying film had been washed off with caustic soda. Our rescue work had obviously not come too soon.

Mainly as a spare-time activity, with occasional help from General Studies classes, we started on the mammoth task of cataloguing and sorting this vast accumulation, wearing protective masks against the fungoid growths on some of the plates. After a year or two, the job was handed over to the Manpower Services Commission, and for three years these gallant men worked steadily through the piles of boxes and transferred their lists to a computer for ease of access.

As the lists grew, we began gradually to realise just how remarkable was the collection: from the 1860s to 1945, here was an almost complete record of many of the School's activities, as well as of changes in the appearance of the town itself.

Among many hundreds of school and house teams, routinely posed in similar ways, we were especially delighted to find photographs of some of the high moments in the School's history, such as visits by British or foreign royalty, prime ministers, archbishops or great generals to lay foundation stones or dedicate fields or new gates. The traditional ceremonies of the school year were there, too: Speech Day cheering, Founder's Day, and Lord's.

Sport figured largely, though there were few action shots, because the slow film speed would not allow these, the Knoll sledging being a welcome exception. Music and drama were represented, the former by the founder members of the Music Society, and by Songs, the latter by various play groups, Speech Day extracts and an innovative house revue.

Patrick Lichfield and Richard Shymansky have brought many of these activities up to date with their modern photographs.

Fashions change, and students of costume can find much to interest them in these pages, especially in the variety of military uniforms. The Harrow "straw" makes an early appearance; and

PHOTO BY RICHARD SHYMANSKY

Jim Golland

beards and moustaches are much in evidence, not only in the masters' groups.

Famous and successful Old Harrovians figure largely, of course, along with many of the masters who helped to establish the School's reputation. It was fascinating to discover familiar faces, such as those of Terence Rattigan or John Mortimer, lurking in youthful guise in group photographs. Gazing at some of the groups inevitably raised questions about the future of the boys concerned: the mass slaughter of the First World War meant that some groups never had a future; but others were distinguished by the number who had made a name for themselves, such as the Grove Cricket XI of 1891, the School Rugby XV of 1937, or the last Sixth Form of Mr Plumptre.

Old Harrovians will feel a sense of nostalgia at the sight of the familiar Ducker, or of other School institutions like Custos, the School custodian. The camera, too, has captured moments of drama such as the West Acre fire, or of beauty with the Hill under snow.

We can see the High Street changing in detail as shopkeepers come and go or shops are demolished, but basically it remains the same, and the familiar view from between Bradbys and The Park looking north appears frequently, giving much of interest for the local historian.

Inevitably, some of the photographic plates being over a hundred years old and not having been preserved in ideal storage conditions, occasional photographs do not have the high quality we expect from modern photography: but they provide us with an irreplaceable record that has been rescued from an ignominious fate.

We have tried to ensure accuracy in our captions by constant checking, but if readers are able to amend details or add information on the identity of people in the groups, we should be delighted to hear from them. What was the "Top Hats v. Bonnets" match of 1902? What lies behind the Head Master's rag group photograph? Who were the members of the cycle corps? If you recognise grandfather, please let us know.

Jim Golland
Former Head of General Studies and Assistant Archivist
1988

Photographic Acknowledgements

PATRICK LICHFIELD
Jacket photographs, front and rear; 129a,b, 130–1, 132a,b.
All Lord Lichfield's photographs are used by courtesy of Kodak.

RICHARD SHYMANSKY
Photos on pages: 5, 7, 19a, 26a, 27, 56, 65b, 94a, 96, 102b, 104a, 105a, 106a,b, 107b, 110b, 111a,b, 113b, 118a, 122–128, 133–160

MANPOWER SERVICES GLASS NEGATIVES
3, 15d, 16, 18b, 20, 21, 22, 23c, 24b, 25, 29, 30a,b, 32, 33d, 34–5, 36, 37b, 38a,b, 40–1, 43, 46b, 47b, 48b, 49, 50a, 55b, 58a,b, 59, 60a, 61a, 63a, 64, 65a, 67, 68a, 69a,b, 70, 71, 74, 75a, 77a, 81, 82, 83b, 84, 86, 88a,b, 89, 90, 93a, 94c, 101a.

HARROW SCHOOL ARCHIVES
12a,b,c,d,e,f,g, 13a,b,c,d,e,f,g, 14a,b,c,d,e, 15a,b,c,e, 16a,b, 17, 18a, 19b, 23a,b, 24a, 26b, 28a,b, 31a,b, 33a,b,c,d, 37a, 39, 40a, 44a,b, 45a,b,c, 46a, 47a, 48a, 50b, 51a,b, 52, 53, 54a,b, 60b, 61b, 62a,b, 63b, 66a,b, 68b,c, 69a, 72a,b, 73, 75b, 76, 77b, 78a,b,c, 79a,b, 80a,b,c, 85, 87, 91a, 93b, 95a,b, 97a,b*, 98a*,b*,c*, 99a*,b,c*, 100a*, 100b,c,d, 101b, 102a, 103a, 104a,b,c, 107a, 108, 109a,b,c, 110a, 112, 113a, 114[2], 115[3], 116[2], 117a[2], 117b, 118b, 119a,b,c.

* From J. S. Armstrong album.
[2] Photo by Sport & General Press Agency.
[3] Photo by Central Press Agency.

MR LASSAM, Fox Talbot Museum
6, 83a.

R. LANGTON DOWN
12d

J. S. GOLLAND
55a

A. C. BACK
70, 71

LONDON NEWS AGENCY (Courtesy Miss Siddons)
91b, 92a,b

SPORT AND GENERAL PRESS AGENCY
114, 116, 117a

CENTRAL PRESS AGENCY
115

HARROW OBSERVER
120–1

KEYSTONE
110a, 112

The map on page 9 was adapted by Vicky Squires from an original by A. F. Venis.

The Publishers would like to thank the Governors of Harrow School, the Head Master, and Mr A. D. K. Hawkyard the School Archivist, for all their co-operation and for permitting the use of photographs from the School archives.

KEY TO MAP (names in capital letters are of School Houses)

1	ELMFIELD	11	THE KNOLL	21	THE HEAD MASTER'S
2	THE GROVE	12	War Memorial	22	MORETONS
3	Leaf Schools (Modern Languages)	13	New Schools	23	Shepherd Churchill Dining Hall
4	Churchill Schools (Computer Suite)	14	Music Schools	24	THE PARK
5	The Copse (English Schools)	15	Old Schools	25	BRADBYS
6	St. Mary's Church	16	Chapel	26	Golf Course
7	Speech Room	17	Peel House	27	Park Lake
8	Art Schools	18	Sports Hall	28	NEWLANDS
9	RENDALLS	19	DRURIES	29	WEST ACRE
10	The Foss	20	Vaughan Library		

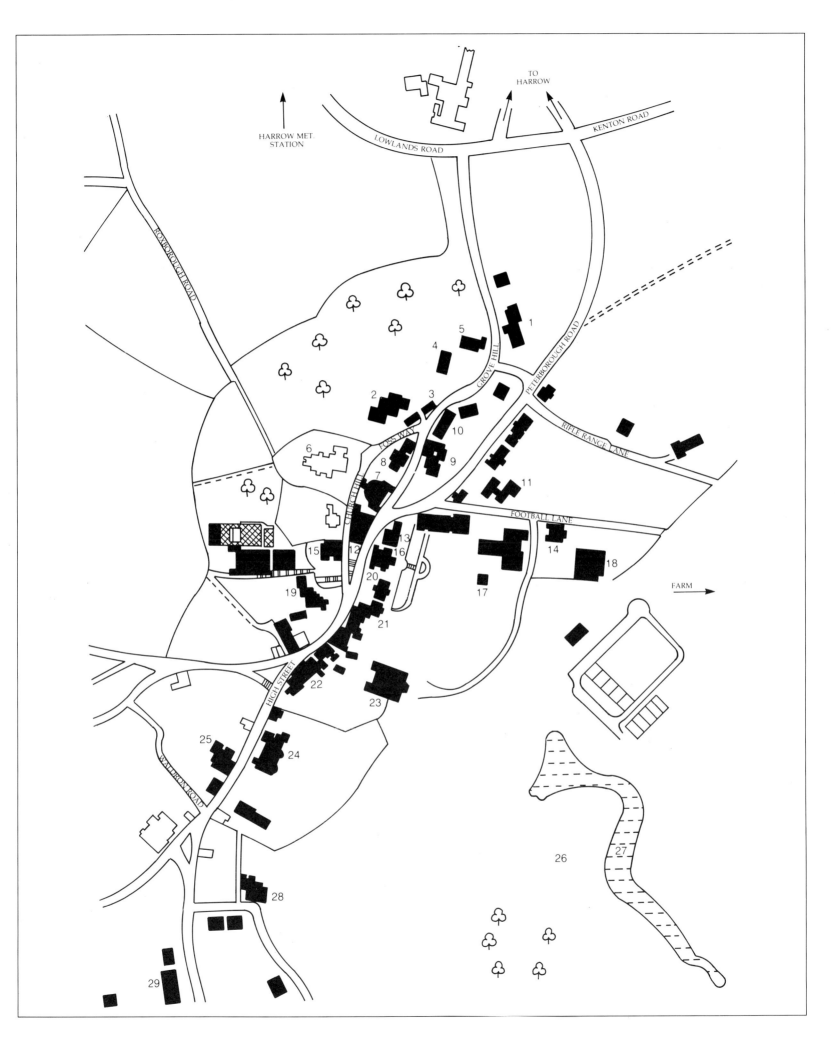

9

THE Fourth Form Room, the original form room of the School dating from 1615, here seen in 1875 but looking much as it does today, with the exception of the curtains used to separate two forms, the gas lighting and the map for a geography lesson.

Amongst the names visible on the oak panels are those of Robert Peel (1800–4), Prime Minister in 1834 and 1841–46, and Anthony Trollope, the novelist (1821–24, 1831–34).

Legend has it that when Warde started to carve his name, he was told to stop as his letters WA were too large. He came back after school and carved the RD, whereupon he was asked to leave: but he broke into the school and carved the final E. Such persistence seemed to foretell a promising future, but little more is known of him.

The School started in September 1615 and the first scholars met in this room. All the lessons for boys of all ages were held in here for at least the first thirty years. In the middle of the seventeenth century, the Head Master moved across the High Street from his room above the Fourth Form Room and the walls in the latter room were panelled in oak. Names were carved on the new panels within a year of their being fitted, and it became the tradition for boys to inscribe their names when they left. Some were carved for them by the School custodian.

Behind the imposing mantelpiece, recent repair work has revealed the original Jacobean fireplace.

REV J. W. Cunningham, Vicar of Harrow 1811–61 and Governor of the School 1818–61. It was probably the evangelical nature of his sermons that prompted the Head Master of the day to remove the boys from the parish church worship and accommodate them in a school chapel, first built in 1839.

MR Jacob Francis Marillier, Mathematics Master 1819–69. The house called Marilliers at 74 High Street was occupied by him. He was appointed Writing Master and the first Librarian of the School in 1826. It was through his French pronunciation of "le Mathematique" that maths at Harrow became known as "Tique". He died in 1876 and was buried in St Mary's, Harrow.

REV William Oxenham, Assistant Master 1826–63 and Housemaster at Moretons for all that time. When the new chapel was being built in 1855 he strongly objected to the idea of having a spire and it was not until after his death in 1863 that one was erected, ironically in his memory.

He was educated at Harrow 1815–19.

SAMUEL Hoare, Custos 1848–85. Not to be confused with the Old Harrovians of the same name. He was a popular and well known figure in the School, and he was variously described as urbane, polite, burly, rubicund, gloomy, rotund, a tyrant to little boys and the living image of Mr Weller, senior. He played cricket (he was Vice-president of the town's club), "ran like a lamplighter" and never mislaid the keys to all the rooms. As "Custos", or Custodian of the School, he superintended the transport of the boys' luggage, rang the bell (with the assistance of "Noggs"), organised the collection for the organ in Chapel and joined the Rifle Corps. There is a brass plate to his memory in the west aisle of the Chapel.

Photo by R. Langton Down.

GEORGE F. Harris, Assistant Master at Harrow 1837–68. Housemaster at The Park 1841–68 and the last Under Master 1864–68. A local JP; the cruciform sun-dial on the Terrace was in his memory. Much respected in local society, he was feared by his pupils but admired by his House: when he went on tours of inspection he sent his butler ahead to warn his boys.

WILLIAM Spottiswoode: one of Harris's first pupils at The Park 1840–42. He took a first class degree in Maths at Balliol in 1846, becoming the University's senior mathematics scholar. He was President of the Royal Society 1878–83 and of the British Association in 1878.

He became famous as a mathematician and physicist.

CHARLES E. Austen-Leigh, Moretons 1846–51; in the Cricket XI 1850–51. Principal Clerk of Committees in the House of Commons.

CAPEL Henry Berger, Moretons 1854–59. He founded the School Musical Society in 1857 and died in 1868. The granite pillars supporting the Chapel gallery are in his memory (see page 14).

ALAN Plantagenet, Viscount Garlies, The Grove 1848–54; Cricket XI 1853–54. Succeeded as 10th Earl of Galloway 1873.

REV Charles John Vaughan, Head Master 1845–59. He brought the numbers in the School up from 69 in 1845 to 466 in 1859. He reformed the monitorial system, and rebuilt the chapel, paying for the chancel out of his own pocket. He also started the English Form for local boys, the precursor of John Lyon School.
   Master of the Temple 1869–94 and Dean of Llandaff 1879–97.

THREE masters whose names were given to the Houses in which they lived.

REV Benjamin Heath Drury. Born in 1817, he entered the School at the age of four and was a Home Boarder 1822–36; Housemaster of Druries 1841–63. He died in 1902.

REV Frederic Rendall, Housemaster at Grove Hill (later Rendalls) 1854–81. Known to his pupils as "Monkey", he was a great scholar but not an inspiring teacher. He died in 1912.

REV Edward Henry Bradby, Housemaster of High Street (later Bradbys) 1853–67. Head Master of Haileybury, and father of several writers, including the social historian, Barbara Hammond. He died in 1893.

RT Hon Sir George Otto Trevelyan, Bt, OM, The Grove 1851–57. An MP, he was an historian, Chancellor of the Duchy of Lancaster and a Governor of the School. He won the prize for an English poem three years running whilst at school. His son, G. M. Trevelyan, was the School's first history specialist, the author of "English Social History," and the biographer of Garibaldi.

A G. Watson, Assistant Master 1854–91. Housemaster, High Street 1868–91.

He was known as "Vanity" Watson, though the reasons for this are disputed: possibly the name came from his love of fancy waistcoats and his impeccable dress sense, though a preacher is said to have called out to him, "All is Vanity," when he was bossily arranging the seating for a chapel service.

As master in charge of "Ducker", the School's open-air swimming pool, he was responsible for its enlargement and modernization.

R EV John Smith, Assistant Master 1854–82. Deeply revered as a most saintly man, he was Rendalls House Tutor and took junior boys in the Fourth Form Room. It was he who fitted the curtains in the room in the photograph on pages 10–11. A true Christian gentleman, he taught the boys to be honest, and developed their characters: though he was not an academic teacher, the boys adored him, and took advantage of his kindness. In a sermon in Chapel, he once declared, "Be upright and you'll always field at cover point in Heaven." Every day he trudged to visit his mother in Pinner, wearing his plaid shawl.

M . Gustave Masson, French Master 1855–88. In charge of the Vaughan Library from 1869 until he died in 1888. He lived at Dame Armstrong's House, on the site of what is now the War Memorial. Very popular and efficient, he had a wide circle of friends and much erudition.

His boyish sense of humour endeared him to many generations."He bubbled with fun and had twinkling eyes," wrote a biographer.

He was a deeply religious man, a keen philologist, and an industrious historian. He would walk five miles to smoke a cigar in seclusion.

F . W. Farrar, Assistant Master 1855–70; Housemaster of The Park 1869–70. After leaving Harrow he became Head Master of Marlborough, Canon and Archdeacon of Westminster, Chaplain to the House of Commons and Dean of Canterbury.

He was the author of "Eric, or Little By Little", and wrote a Life of Christ and a Life of St Paul.

Keenly intellectual, he inspired in the boys a love of geography and natural history.

T HE School Musical Society c. 1858. Second from left on the back row is Capel Berger, who founded the Society. Extreme right in the back row is J. A. Cruikshank, Head of the School in 1859 and an Assistant Master 1866–91. He was Housemaster at Church Hill (now the site of the War Memorial) 1877–1891. His special care was the tending of the Terrace gardens, and seats to his memory can be found at the top of the Terrace steps.

JOHN E. Bourchier, Head Master's 1858–63. Head of the School in 1862, he died in 1866.

The Bourchier History and Reading Prizes are in his memory.

EDWARD Ernest Bowen, Assistant Master 1859–1901, Housemaster at The Grove 1881–1901. The author of "Forty Years On", he was passionately keen on football and closely concerned with the early years of the Football Association.

A remarkable man in many ways, he was also a fanatical walker, having walked in his youth from Cambridge to Oxford in less than twenty-four hours. He had a collection of maps showing that he had walked round the entire coast line of England. He was responsible for the introduction of "torpids", the junior house football game, in 1873, and for "Cricket Bill", a form of registration on the field that stopped boys having to climb the hill for roll call in the middle of a match, as previously had been the case.

A colleague wrote of him: "Behind the word-fencing, the straw-splitting, the blithesome jests, the brilliant paradoxes,

and the apparent levity...there ran the deep under-current of the most earnest and serious, the most true and tender of natures. What devotion to duty there was in him, what sincerity, what purity, what open-handedness, what magnanimity!"

His nickname was "Sleuth", from his power of investigating mysteries; and his special interests included astronomy and military history. He had walked behind the German armies in the Franco–Prussian War and his lectures on those battles were particularly vivid and long remembered by his pupils.

He died pushing his cycle up a hill whilst on a touring holiday in France.

DR Henry Montagu Butler, (Head Master's 1846–51): one of Dr Vaughan's brightest students and Head of the School, he returned to Harrow at 26 as Head Master from 1860 to 1885. He was appointed the following year Master of Trinity College, Cambridge. With Dr Vaughan (page 13) he was largely responsible for the growth of the School and its great reputation as a scholastic establishment.

ONE of the oldest photographs in the School: the School Football team of 1859.

The Captain is J. A. Cruikshank (see opposite).

Left on centre row is J. T. Prior, the barrister who lived at The Red House, Middle Road, Harrow: he helped found the Harrow Building Society and was the brother of E. S. Prior, architect of the Music Schools.

MRS H. Montagu Butler, wife of the Head Master. Née Miss Georgina Elliott of Sudbury, she married in 1861 and died in 1883.

She presented the eagle lectern in Chapel in 1862 and a new school bell in 1882.

A composite photograph of 224 boys in the School, 1863, taken by Goshawk, the School's official photographer, taxidermist and hairdresser.

THE School Cricket XI in 1860, the first year the match against Eton was drawn. From left to right, standing, are: H. R. T. ALEXANDER, Captain the following year; R. D. WALKER, one of a famous family of cricketing brothers from Southgate*; A. W. T. DANIEL, Captain of the XI, who scored 112 in the match; R. H. L. BURTON; R. D. H. ELPHINSTONE, skilled at off-drives; A. J. MCNEILE; VISCOUNT ACHESON, the 4th Earl Gosford; and W. FULLER-MAITLAND, who was to be in the XI for another three years and who represented Oxford University at cricket, rackets and athletics as well as being in the School football team.

Seated, from left to right, are: I. D. WALKER, brother of R.D.†; G. UPCHER; and G. H. FILLINGHAM, later President of Notts County Cricket Club.

*R. D. Walker excelled in many sports and was said to be the best batsman on a difficult wicket that Harrow had produced; he was Captain of the School Football XI in 1860, School Rackets Champion and an Oxford rackets player for four years; he played cricket for the University for five years and played for the Gentlemen v. Players whilst still at university.

†I. D. Walker was Captain of the XI in 1862–63, Captain of the Harrow Wanderers (the touring team of former pupils) from 1870 to 1897, and Captain of Middlesex CCC. He was said to have been one of the best timers of fast bowling ever encountered.

16

A group of Harrovians on the steps of the Old Schools *c.* 1865.
One of the earliest photographs of the Harrow straw hat.

B OYS, perhaps attracted by Byronic legends, studying their books by the Peachey stone *c.* 1865. This was the grave of John Peachey (of Harrow and the West Indies) on which Byron used to lie to compose verses.

T HE School Cricket XI, in 1866. At Lord's that year, Harrow won by an innings and 136 runs, dismissing Eton for 42 in the second innings. Sitting on the left, holding the match-winning ball, is Frank Cobden, who took 8 for 47. At the rear, holding a bat, is the other hero of the day, Walter Money of Bradbys, who took 9 wickets for 50 runs. He became Captain of the XI in the following year and Captain of the Cambridge University XI in 1870.

Cobden was the bowler of what one spectator described as the "most thrilling over ever bowled" in the University match in 1870: he took the last three Oxford wickets in the last three balls of the match, enabling Cambridge to win by two runs.

Money was famed for his slow underhand bowling; after he left school, he became one of the finest batsmen in English cricket.

THE Sixth Form cricket ground in 1874, with a young barrow boy resting from his labours. Field House is to the right of the Old Schools, in the centre of the picture.

A. J. Webbe, in 1872, one of the cricketing "Giants of Old". He was Captain of the XI in 1874, Captain of the Oxford University Cricket XI 1877–78, and for many years Captain of Middlesex CCC. He toured Australia in 1878. In July 1888 he was amateur tennis champion.

THE Old Schools in 1875 showing the Crown and Anchor Inn on the left, with the balcony. As its landlord for many generations was a member of the Bliss family, it was known to Harrow boys as the "The Abode of Bliss". Having a public house so close to the school room was a constant source of concern for the authorities, and it was eventually moved to a new site at the top of West Street.

Dame Armstrong's House on the right was free of the creepers that obscured it in later photographs.

THE High Street in 1875, showing the original front gardens to nos. 34–40, just before extensions were built.

The White Hart Inn is on the extreme left. Gieves & Hawkes' present property is occupied here by a corn chandler's.

HARROW boys with rather restless local children in front of the Old Schools, 1875.
LEFT.

NOT the inmates of a prison working party, but the School Football XI, 1878, in the regulation costume.

THE High Street before 1880, when the present fountain was erected at the top of West Street: the old well winding gear can still be seen under its ornate cover. This well was probably the town's main water supply.

The shops include those of John Craker, shoemaker; William Overhead, bookseller and printer of "The Harrow Gazette"; George Clarke, grocer; and James Chatham, shoemaker.

Most of the shops in the High Street owed their existence to the patronage of the School.

H. O. D. Davidson, Assistant Master 1878–1913.

He was in charge of Garlands when Churchill arrived in 1888, and moved from High Street to open the new house of Elmfield in 1893.

REAR view of the Chapel from the Head Master's orchard *c.* 1880. The New Schools (1855) are on the right.

A group of boys from The Knoll enjoy a somewhat precarious sledge ride in 1881.

THE Head Master's House seen from Church Hill in the last century. The "Penfold" letter box suggests a fairly early date, perhaps in the 1880s. On the right, notice boards grace the gates of the School Yard; beyond is a weather-boarded house formerly occupied by Custos on the site of the old Crown and Anchor hostelry.

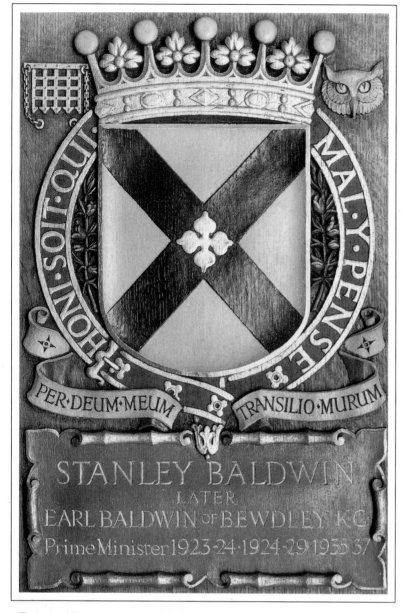

HAROLD Joachim (Head Master's 1882–86). The School's first Balliol Scholar, 1886. Author, and Fellow of Merton College, Oxford; he taught T. S. Eliot philosophy in 1914. He was Professor of Logic at Oxford 1919–35.

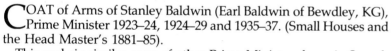

COAT of Arms of Stanley Baldwin (Earl Baldwin of Bewdley, KG), Prime Minister 1923–24, 1924–29 and 1935–37. (Small Houses and the Head Master's 1881–85).

This and six similar ones of other Prime Ministers hang in Speech Room, along with the emblems of other Old Harrovians who have made their marks in their chosen professions.

THE Harrow fire brigade seen in front of The Park in 1883. A fine collection of beards is in evidence.

HEAD Master's House Football XI 1884. 2nd from left, seated, is Stanley Baldwin (Prime Minister 1923; 1924–28; 1935–37). Centre of the rear rank is the Captain, Edward Montagu Butler, son of the Head Master and later an Assistant Master and Housemaster at The Park.

He was Captain of the School Football XI in 1884 and of Cricket in 1885. He was Amateur Rackets Champion in 1889, having won the Public Schools Rackets title with Buxton in 1884 and Crawley in 1885. He helped found the Harrow Association and was its chairman in 1928.

COL the Rt Hon Sir Francis Stanley Jackson, GCSI, GCIE, (Head Master's 1884–89). Captain of the School Cricket XI 1889, of Cambridge University Cricket XI 1892–93, and of England 1905. One of the greatest cricketers the School has produced, he was President of the MCC in 1921 and a School Governor 1923–27 and 1939–47 (Chairman 1942–46).

THE Masters in artistic poses in July 1885, the last term of the Head Master, Dr H. Montagu Butler, who is seen clutching his gloves in the centre of the picture. He had just been appointed Dean of Gloucester, and was to become Master of Trinity College, Cambridge, the following year.

THE High Street under snow in 1885. J. Woodbridge is shown as the licensee of the Crown and Anchor at the top of West Street.

A man shows off his new tricycle in the High Street in 1886. It is to be hoped he did not try riding it up the hill. H. R. Seward was now the licensee of the Crown and Anchor.

A rather bleak corridor in The Park in 1887. It is interesting to see that names as far back as 1839 are carved on the boards that line the walls.

THE interior of The Park in 1887. Angels appear to be tying up their shoelaces on either side of Venus, while full decanters await a select party of guests.

31

HILLS & Saunders' shop at 104 High Street, past the King's Head, in 1887. They had taken over from Goshawks as the official School photographers and are still operating in West Street today.

R OBERT Somervell, Assistant Master 1887–1933. Bursar 1888–1919; Housemaster of West Acre 1904–11.

It was he who taught English to Winston Churchill and whom Winston so admired for his instruction in the formation of an English sentence.

T HE splendid physiognomy of Sir Arthur Fenton Hort, Assistant Master 1888–1922 and Housemaster of Newlands 1905–22. He took over as master in charge of Ducker in 1891 when A. G. Watson retired (see p. 14). It was he who reported Winston Churchill for "swimming twice in one day".

B RIAN Piers Lascelles, Assistant Master 1885–1901; Librarian 1888–1914; Curator of the Butler Museum 1905–22. Known as "The Magdalen Giant", he is said to have been at least 6' 10½" in height; stories about him are numerous. Boys reported that he could reach the top shelves in the Library without using the steps, and he would often peer over the top of the door on entering a form-room, which the boys found unnerving. He was one of two masters who introduced Science into the School.

He also found time to index all the names carved on panels in the Fourth Form Room.

A Small House group in 1889: The Rev. E. Gilliat at Byron House with his wife, dog, family and boarders. He was a writer of historical novels.

A familiar sight to Harrow boys: Brightwell's butcher's shop in Peterborough Road in 1889. Young Winston would have passed here on his afternoon rambles. Brightwell's also had a branch at 23 High Street, which is still a butcher's shop today.

Hygiene was obviously not a consideration when this picture was taken.

MAIDMENT'S draper's shop at 3 High Street in 1890. The wrought-iron balconies are still to be seen, as well as part of the shop fittings, although this is now part of the Head Master's House. Undergarments and socks entice customers in the right-hand window, while on the left the prices are certainly attractive today.

A notice in the window announces that the shop will be closed on Wednesdays during the vacation, when presumably trade dropped to a minimum.

This shop was later the Hill Tea House.

THE servants employed by F. E. Marshall at Newlands in 1890 shortly after it opened.

AN attractive winter scene across what is now the golf course, taken from the garden of Kennet House in Harrow Park in the 1890s. The Head Master's House is in the middle of the picture, and the spires of St Mary's Church and the School Chapel can be seen on the right.

THE King's Head Assembly
Rooms and the local fire
station, shortly after the latter
was built, about 1890. A bearded
fireman proudly displays the
latest in fire-fighting equipment,
including, probably, the turn-
table ladders seen forming a
triumphal arch in the 1912 picture welcoming George V, on
page 77.

A splendidly ornate fitting
encloses the bell on the roof,
and a board on the window
announces that inside are also
the Local Board Offices: the local
Education Office was here until
the 1960s.

Part of the Assembly Rooms
building is given over to shops,
one of which is to let. The "livery
and bait" stables merely provide
food for horses, not uniforms or
fishing requisites.

AN undated photo of the
Vaughan Library and a Kil-
burn Brewery horse and cart.
The northern wing of the Head
Master's House is seen on the
right.

DUCKER in the 1890s. The former open-air swimming pool, 500 feet long and one of the largest in Europe.

It took its name from the fact that it had formally been a duck-pond, not because boys could duck each other in it, though it was here that Churchill was in trouble for pushing in Leo Amery, who was at the time a Monitor.

THE Old Schools from The Vaughan Library *c.* 1890. The Crown and Anchor Inn has gone and in its place are Winkley, the tailor, and Owen, the pastry cook and confectioner. These buildings were demolished in 1929 (see page 20).

THE view from the Terrace in 1890, showing many differences from the scene today. The Old Schools appear over the heads of the two industrious students; the Chapel has no transepts (1902–3); the blinds are on Ivy House (now the site of the War Memorial); the ivy-covered New Schools have not yet received their extensions of 1914 or 1923; and below Speech Room can be seen a flight of steps where now can be found the Science Schools of 1934.

THE School Army Corps forming square on the Terrace, 1891, probably including Winston Churchill. In the background, the Head Master's House and the Vaughan Library, both almost submerged in ivy; and in front of the latter, a bevy of school photographers. Many of these boys would subsequently have fought in the Boer War.

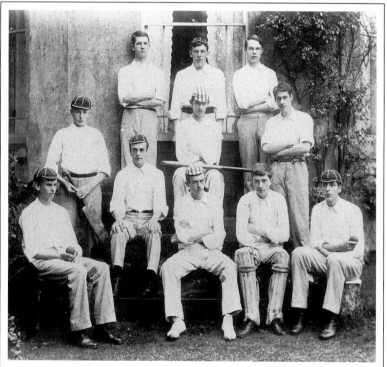

Rendalls House seen from the west before the building of the Art Schools, *c.* 1890. The gardens belonged to The Grove.

A distinguished Eleven. The Grove House Cricket XI of 1891: the team includes a future Housemaster, two generals, two who were created CMG, five awarded DSO, two CB, one CBE and one MC.

Standing at rear are: LT COL R. W. BRADLEY DSO; MAJ GEN J. W. SANDILANDS, CB, CMG, DSO, GOC China 1929–33; and F. L. D. ELLIOTT, CB, Assistant Commissioner of the Metropolitan Police.

Standing in the centre are: LT COL A. L. MOULTON-BARRETT, DSO, Croix-de-Guerre; MAJOR F. POPE, DSO; and R. MCG. LAIRD, CBE, shipbuilder.

Seated in front are: BRIG GEN C. S. ROME, CMG, DSO, Captain of School Cricket XI 1893, Public Schools middle-weight boxing champion 1893, and Captain of Sandhurst Cricket and Football XIs, Officer Commanding Royal Welch Fusiliers 1915–17; C. G. POPE, Captain of School Cricket XI 1891 (when he took 7 wickets at Lord's and helped Harrow to victory), Assistant Master at Harrow 1899–1929; Housemaster at Church Hill 1912–15 and at The Grove 1915–29; R. C. TREVELYAN, son of Rt Hon Sir G. O. Trevelyan and an author and poet; H. LEFROY, and H. R. YORKE, MC.

44

THE Head Master's House Group of 1891 (Rev J. E. C. Welldon).
Winston Churchill is on the extreme left, peeping behind the
pillar, as usual finding an isolated position in the group.

YOUNG Winston Churchill at
School: although this is the
type of photograph normally
taken when boys leave school,
for them to present to friends
and masters, this would seem to
have been taken in his first year
or two at the School. He looks
particularly handsome and ele-
gant with his Eton collar and tie
pin.

A typical Small House group: the boys in Mr E. W. Howson's house at Hillside, Peterborough Road, in 1892. Mr Howson, standing behind his wife and child, was the composer of the School Song, "Here, Sir!" and co-author with G. T. Warner of one of the early histories of the School. He died in 1905 and the Terrace steps are in his memory. He was Housemaster of Druries 1894–1905.

THE Middlesex Rifle Volunteers, 1892. These fierce-looking local warriors can be seen on page 61 lining the streets in 1902.

THE School Shooting VIII of 1893, with their fierce, moustachioed instructor. The rifles appear to be fitted with Morris tubes, for practice firing, possibly on the Milling Ground below the School Yard.

THE High Street in 1893 as Winston Churchill would have known it. The shops from left to right are: Miss Armstrong's Fancy Repository (a haberdasher); W. Meades, the fishmonger; J. Wright Cooper, the bakery and tea shop patronised by young Winston; Conway & Son, tailors; Stephen Hartley, chemist; and Alfred Powell, shoemaker. The Crown and Anchor Inn, at the top of West Street, was being run by G. Tyler.

THE rear of the old Knoll.

SAMUEL John Gurney Hoare, Viscount Templewood (The Head Master's 1894–99). He played rackets and tennis for Oxford University, became an MP, and, as Sir Samuel Hoare, was Foreign Secretary in 1935.

He was a School Governor 1947–48.

THE Head Master's House in the 1890s, with, on the left, the Chapel and its former west door. As the dust and noise used to enter easily from this direction, it was decided to change the position of the door and build a porch in 1902–3, with money raised for the Boer War memorial.

THE Vaughan Library: an un-
dated photograph *c.* 1900.
The painting "Black Monday",
now in the Old Speech Room
Gallery, can be seen on the left.
George Richmond's portrait of
Dr Vaughan is in the centre of
the far wall. It now adorns the
Old Harrovians' Room.

HEAD Master's House
Cricket XI 1899. The Cap-
tain in the blazer is Sir Samuel
John Gurney Hoare, Viscount
Templewood, Foreign Secretary
1935.

THE Head Master's House O.T.C. squad in 1899, in their Hussars' uniforms. 40 per cent of these boys died on active service in either the Boer War or the Great War.

C. A. Vine, Bandmaster 1898–1908. When he was appointed there were twelve boys in the band; by 1902 there were forty-four in two bands.

51

CHAMPION Shooting Pair 1899: F. E. Bray (left) and H. S. Green, both of Church Hill House. Bray was Captain of the School Shooting VIII 1899–1901, won the Spencer Cup at Bisley in 1899 and became President of the Cambridge Union. He won the Military Cross.

Green was Captain of the VIII in 1902 and was killed in action in 1917.

THE School Rifle Corps ready for inspection on the Terrace lawn, beside the new Butler Museum, built in 1886.

THE Harrow Masters in 1898, just before the departure of the Head Master, Rev James Edward Cowell Welldon, to be Bishop of Calcutta. Just under half of them have decided to follow the Head Master's lead in wearing their mortarboards for the photographs.

In the front row are H. O. D. DAVIDSON (Churchill's first Housemaster at Garlands and later at Elmfield 1893–1913); C. COLBECK (Housemaster at Moretons 1890–1903 and a prime mover in the provision of the Harrow Recreation Ground in Pinner Road); G. H. HALLAM (Housemaster at The Park 1887–1906); W. D. BUSHELL (Housemaster at Rendalls 1881–98, Chaplain 1899 and C.O. of the School Corps 1884–91 – and possessor of the finest beard in the picture); E. E. BOWEN (Housemaster at The Grove 1881–1901, author of "Forty Years On", and donor of The Grove and The Copse to the School), (see p. 15); The Head Master 1885–98; R. BOSWORTH SMITH (Housemaster at The Knoll 1867–1901 and author); A. C. TOSSWILL (Housemaster at High Street 1878–91; winner of the inter-university long jump 1868 and a skilled mountain climber); F. E. MARSHALL (Housemaster at Newlands 1889–1904); and J. W. W. WELSFORD (Housemaster at Bradbys 1893–1904).

The hatless, handsome figure behind Mr Bowen is R. SOMERVELL, whom Churchill praised for his teaching of English grammatical structure. Next to him, behind the Head Master, is F. C. SEARLE (Housemaster at The Head Master's and Commanding Officer of the O.T.C., later Housemaster at Moretons); second from left in the back row is C. H. P. "PIGGY" MAYO (Housemaster at The Knoll 1909–1919 and the master who taught Churchill maths.) At the extreme right in that row is B. P. LASCELLES (see page 33): presumably he is standing on the ground, though the others in his row are on benches.

THE School Cricket XI in 1899. The Captain in the centre is E. M. Dowson, who was in the XI 1895–99 and Captain 1898–99. He went on to captain the Cambridge University XI in 1903 and the Surrey Cricket XI. In 1897 he had shared in a 200 partnership with T. S. O. Cole, whose 142 was the School's highest score against Eton.

In the 1898 match Dowson had taken nine wickets for 127 runs and scored 47 in a nine-wicket victory. The match in 1899 was drawn, but he scored 87 not out and took 6 for 108. In five matches at Lord's he took 35 wickets in all, a hard record to beat.

THE Butler Museum *c.* 1900. Now the Careers Centre.

THE School bugle band in 1900, resplendent in their Hussars' uniforms (see page 62).

THE local hunt meets at the King's Head in 1900. Mr G. Brown is the landlord of the ancient hostelry and next door is the Harrow Toilet Club (the hairdresser's). Between that and Nash & Luxton's piano warehouse are Winkley & Baldry, tailors.

On the left a small errand boy confidently carries his wares in a basket on his head. Behind him stands a diminutive Harrovian in an Eton collar. On the extreme right, at 43 High Street, is the shop of William Oglesby, silk mercer and draper, who advertised for sale "Lace sets, mob caps, frillins, hats, bonnets, gloves, ribbons, flags and fancy drapery of every kind."

THE front of The Grove in 1901, at the time of the death of its famous Housemaster, E. E. Bowen, author of "Forty Years On".

THE Grove seen from Rendalls in 1901, looking over the remains of the old hanging garden of The Grove, now the site of the 1913 extension of the Art Schools. The cottage on the right was used before the last war to store gardening tools.

THE Head Master's House Group in 1901 (Dr Wood). The photo-graph includes two sons of the King of Siam and in the second row from the back, 4th from the right, Hon John Vereker, 6th Viscount Gort, VC, who was Commander-in-Chief of the British Expeditionary Forces in France in 1939–40.

THE members of the Philathletic Club in 1902, seen in merry mood. To this club, formed in 1853, are elected the leading figures in the School's many games teams.

"TOP HATS v. Bonnets": a football match with a difference in 1902.

SPEECH Day 1902: Field-Marshal Earl Roberts of Kandahar walking down Church Hill to the Chapel to lay the foundation stone of the new transepts, to be erected in memory of those who died in the Boer War. Escorted by the Head Master, Rev Joseph Wood, he can be distinguished by his white plumed hat. The southern porch of the Chapel was built later as part of the same reconstruction.

The shops on the left were demolished in 1929. The building in the centre, almost swamped in creepers, is Dame Armstrong's House, now the site of the War Memorial terrace. Behind it is the house known as Church Hill.

FIELD-MARSHALL Earl Roberts of Kandahar in 1902, laying the foundation stone of the Chapel transepts.

ELMFIELD House Group 1902. The Housemaster is H. O. D. Davidson: he was Churchill's first Housemaster when in charge of Garlands in 1888. The Hon Viscount Anson, 4th Earl of Lichfield, is on the Housemaster's right, holding the cup. He was the grandfather of the present Earl.

THE bugle band of the Harrow OTC in 1903 in changed uniforms (see page 55). They had silver-plated instruments and lightweight aluminium drums, donated by local residents. The Head Master had contributed the leopard skin.

THE Coade stone lion on the east face of The Park, before it was moved in 1906 by E. M. Butler to its present position on the High Street frontage.

A room in Northwick Lodge (which was lower down Peterborough Hill than Garlands). When this photograph was taken in 1904, it was occupied by C. W. Mercer (later Dornford Yates, the novelist.)

S PEECH Day 1905: King Edward VII and Queen Alexandra arriving in the rain. The newly built south porch on the Chapel is now visible. The King went on to open the new sports field that had been bought by subscription to preserve the open spaces from the hands of speculative builders.

In the picture, the band are on the lawn of the Vaughan Library and the street is lined by the School O.T.C. in their Hussars' uniforms.

In spite of the weather, the date was June 30th.

In honour of this visit, E. W. Howson wrote a new School Song, *Avete*. Its first verse ran:

Shine out, fair Sun, today upon the Hill!
    Clash, Bells, from yon grey spire,
    And o'er the verdant shire
With jubilant peal the summer breezes fill!
    Deck out the winding street
    With fluttering pennons gay,
As young and old in thousands haste to greet
    The King, the King,
The King of England passing by today.

THE Science Schools (of 1874) seen before a new floor was added in 1914. On the left in the distance is Rendalls; on the right the Butler Museum, designed by Basil Champneys and opened in 1886. The lawns seem to be producing a larger crop of daisies than would be tolerated by today's gardeners.

THE view from the Terrace in 1905, before the erection of the stone balustrades in memory of R. Bosworth-Smith (The Knoll Housemaster 1867–1901; died 1908) or the stone steps in memory of E. W. Howson (Druries Housemaster 1894–1905 and author of "Here, Sir!").

From left to right: the Vaughan Library, Old Schools, Chapel (with the new porch and transepts), New Schools and Speech Room (see pages 40–41).

THE School Cricket XI v. The Old Harrovians, 1906. This historic photograph includes such great names of Harrow cricket as F. S. Jackson, M. C. Kemp, E. M. Dowson and A. J. Webbe.

CHURCH Hill House: Champion Glee singers 1906. (Housemaster: J. C. Moss).

G. E. V. Crutchley (left at rear) was also in the School teams for cricket, rackets and fives. G. H. Palmer (seated left) was in the School Gym VIII; and E. H. Crake (seated right) was Captain of the School Cricket XI in 1905–6 and a School fives player. C. P. Moodie (extreme right, rear) was killed in action in the Great War and L. C. Robinson (centre, rear) was torpedoed three times in that same conflict.

Church Hill House was formerly on the site of the War Memorial. It was open from 1846–1915.

THE Head Master's House Group, 1907 (Rev J. Wood). The master to the right of the Head Master is Rev Edgar Stogdon (West Acre 1884–89; Assistant Master 1903–7). On the left of Dr Wood is Sir J. R. M. Butler, son of the former Head Master, H. Montagu Butler. He became Regius Professor of Modern History at Cambridge and official historian of the Second World War. A younger brother, killed on active service, is in the second row from the back, second from the left. Fifth from the right in that same row is Pandit Nehru, Prime Minister of India in 1947. BELOW.

THE School Cycle Corps, 1907. When these first appeared, they were greeted with the cry, "See the monkey on the gridiron!"

F. A. Leaf, Elmfield 1904–9, Housemaster of West Acre 1926–39; father of J. F. Leaf (Senior Master 1983–88).

G. H. Morrison, Elmfield 1903–8, a member of the School Football XI in 1907, seen in his football shirt. He was killed in action in 1915.

HEAD Master's House Cricket XI 1907. Hon H. R. Alexander is second from the left in back row. (Field-Marshal Earl Alexander of Tunis, KG, GCB, OM, GCMG, CSI, DSO, MC; Commander-in-Chief Middle East 1942–43; C-in-C Mediterranean 1944–45; Governor-General of Canada 1946; School Governor 1952–62).

His bust can be seen in the War Memorial, and his Coat of Arms in Speech Room, where it was installed in 1987. He died in 1969.

THE Harrow and Eton Rugby XVs on March 12th, 1907, when Eton won the first inter-school rugby match ever played at Harrow. Rugby had been introduced in 1903 and was played in the Easter term for a few years. It was dropped in 1911, when Eton won by 29–3, but restarted in 1927 under Dr Norwood.

The Harrow XV are in dark shirts.

WEST Acre after the disastrous fire of April, 1908. Only the shell stands.

THE HARROW FIRE
APRIL 4TH 1908.
11 P.M.

WEST Acre seen later in 1908, miraculously restored to normality.

CONTEMPORARY postcards showing the house on fire and the rescue workers outside the still smoking building on the following day.

Photos by Mr Gifford of Roxeth, from the collection of Mr A. C. Back.

THE Head Master's House tug-of-war team, 1908.

C. W. Fladgate, Elmfield 1904–8. Major-General 1942; Director of Signals at the War Office 1942–43; ADC to the King 1941–46.

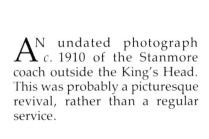

AN undated photograph c. 1910 of the Stanmore coach outside the King's Head. This was probably a picturesque revival, rather than a regular service.

OFFICERS in the School's Officer Training Corps in 1910, wearing black armbands in mourning for King Edward VII. Seated on the extreme left is Hon H. R. L. G. Alexander (later Earl Alexander of Tunis).

THE Harrow Masters in 1910. Among them are some of the Masters who taught Churchill. The Head Master, Rev Dr Joseph Wood, MVO, was about to retire from Harrow, to become Canon of Rochester Cathedral.

In the front row, left to right, are: B. P. Lascelles ("the Magdalen Giant"); L. M. Moriarty; R. Somervell; H. O. D. Davidson (Churchill's first Housemaster); The Head Master; J. C. Moss; E. Graham; M. C. Kemp and Rev E. C. E. Owen.

The figure in the straw hat at the rear is J. H. Titchener, (Custos 1885–1924).

DR Lionel Ford, Head Master 1910–25. He was chiefly instrumental in the building of the War Memorial, and his coat of arms may be seen there in his memorial window.

AN extract from "Twelfth Night" was presented on Speech Day, 1911. From left to right, the actors are M. G. DAVIDSON, Head of the School, as Fabian; R. F. GORE-BROWNE as Maria; C. E. H. LOXTON as Sir Andrew Aguecheek; G. P. CABLE as a hatted Olivia; R. E. M. DAVIDSON, smiling and cross-gartered as Malvolio; and G. E. WAKEFIELD as Sir Toby Belch. Gore-Browne was "an amusing if somewhat muscular Maria"; Loxton "showed his genius for farce"; Davidson jun. was "far from disappointing" as Malvolio and used as a prop the same letter used by his uncle in the part in 1864. Cable had four parts on Speech Day and was excellent as Olivia.

Cable and Loxton were killed in action in the Great War; Gore-Browne was wounded and taken prisoner; Wakefield and the two Davidsons were all wounded or invalided out. M. G. Davidson was the son of H. O. D. Davidson (see page 75).

THE triumphal arch erected near The King's Head in 1912 for the visit of King George V and Queen Mary.

The message refers to an earlier visit by King Edward VII in 1905 (see page 64). The arch is constructed from a pair of firemen's ladders. Streamers, garlands and flags proliferate, and the town has a festive air. Two mounted policemen appear to be escorting away a motorcyclist and his sidecar passenger.

ASWEWELCOMED
THE FATHER.
SO WE WELCOME
THE SON

KING George V on the Chapel
steps in 1912.

BRADBY'S Cricket XI in 1912. Standing with the ball is Vivian Elgood (1906–12) (see front cover photograph).

THE Matriarch. This grand old lady, seen in 1912, was Mrs Sandwith, of The Woodlands, Harrow, wife of General J. P. Sandwith and mother of four boys who were at the School 1867–8.

SCHOOL Servants Cricket XI 1914.

NEWLANDS House Group in 1911 (Sir Arthur Hort, Bt, 1905–22). Lady Hort sits beneath an imposing hat.

HOME Boarders, 1915, with some splendid centre-partings. Far fewer boys today board at home, during the term.

ANDREW B. Philp (The Knoll 1912–17) winning the high jump in the School Sports in 1916. The following year he broke the Public Schools' high jump record at 5'9".

GUY Butler breaks the tape in the 200 yards race, *c.* 1916. (For biographical details see page 82.)
Photo presented by Major Sir Charles Buchanan (The Knoll, 1913–17).

CHAMPION Corps Squad: The Grove, 1916.
Sir Lancelot Royle (centre) represented England in the Olympic Games of 1924, and was a School Governor 1948–62.

THE Park House Group in 1916. The Housemaster is E. M. BUTLER, son of the former Head Master, H. Montagu Butler. His son, GUY, the Olympic athlete, is third from left in a white blazer, seated holding a tankard. Others in the group (apart from the dog) bear some well-known Harrovian surnames such as BRIG C. H. GURNEY (back row, 1st left), CAPT E. G. HOYER MILLAR (back row, 3rd left), LT CDR P. H. PLEYDELL-BOUVERIE (back row, 4th left), and CAPT O. C.

BRIDGEMAN, MC (seated, extreme left). The Head of House (with arms folded to left of the Housemaster) is A. V. D. HORT, son of Sir Arthur Hort, Housemaster of Newlands from 1905 to 1922.

E. M. Butler was Housemaster 1906–19; it was he who moved the Coade stone lion from the east face of The Park to its present location in the High Street (see page 63).

THE Monitors in 1917. Head of the School, in the centre of the front row, is Guy Butler, grandson of Dr H. Montagu Butler (Head Master 1860–85) and one of the School's greatest athletes. He was at The Park 1913–18, and was Captain of the School Cricket XI and Football XI in 1917 and of the School Association Football XI in 1917–18, Victor Ludorum 1916–18, President of the Cambridge University Athletics Club, finalist in the Olympic Games in 1920 and 1924 (winning a gold medal for the 4×400 relay in 1920), and a world record holder for the 300 yards in 1927.

CECIL Beaton, photographer and stage designer, seen when at School. He was at Bradbys 1918–22.
Photo by courtesy of Mr Lassam of Fox Talbot Museum.

SHOPS at the top of West Street at the end of the first world war. The signpost indicates the way to South Harrow Station and, in the other direction, to the Metropolitan and Great Central Station.

84

THE Archbishop of Canterbury (Dr Randall Davidson, Moretons, 1862–1867) laying the foundation stone of the War Memorial on 6 October 1921. The architect was Sir Herbert Baker.

Church Hill House and Ivy House still stand in this picture, though Dame Armstrong's has gone.

A young Harrovian with his family at Lord's in 1923.

THE crowds on Speech Day 1923, showing the scaffolding for the extension to New Schools.

SPEECH Day 1924. Cheering on the steps by the north door of Speech Room.

THE Outcasts' Cricket XI in
outlandish pose in 1924. This
team is restricted to boys in their
last year at school who are not in
the First XI, and usually includes
at least three masters, who provide the transport to matches.

THE Head Master's Rag
Group in 1927. One of many
photographs that can probably
be explained only by the partici-
pants.

A wedding group in the Pope family at The Grove, 1925. The Housemaster, C. G. Pope, is standing second from the right (see page 44).

THE School Rugby XV in 1927, when Dr Norwood brought about the revival of this sport as one of the School games. The game had been abandoned as a School sport in 1911 after five defeats in a row by Eton; in 1927 Eton also won, by 33–6. D. G. I. A. Gordon (4th Marquess of Aberdeen and Temair; died 1974) was the captain. The full-back was K. R. M. Carlisle, who became a School Governor 1966–76.

HOME Boarders and Small Houses Rugby XV, 1928. Extreme left in the front row is John D. Profumo (1928–33), Secretary of State for War 1960–63.

A trilby-hatted press photographer watches the Duchess of York and The Head Master, Dr Cyril Norwood, enter the School Yard guarded by a mounted policeman. Behind them follows the Duke of York, later King George VI. The year is 1929 and cloche hats are still the rage with the ladies.

Photo: London News Agency. Reproduced by courtesy of Miss Siddons.

THE Head Master accompanies the Duke and Duchess of York up Church Hill in 1929. The space behind them had only recently been cleared of shops, revealing Druries and the Old Schools for the first time.

Photo: London News Agency. Reproduced by courtesy of Miss Siddons.

THE Head Master escorts the Duke and Duchess of York from the Old Schools during their visit in 1929. Photography is still popular with the boys, as it was in 1890 (see page 42).

Photo: London News Agency. Reproduced by courtesy of Miss Siddons.

THE cast of Mr T. F. Coade's production of "Macbeth" in 1929. Macbeth was played by HUGH SAUNDERS (LT COL H. N. SAUNDERS, OBE, TD, barrister and company director; The Knoll, 1924–29) who "never faltered and showed remarkable emotional fervour" according to the reviewer. Lady Macbeth, showing "thorough mastery and understanding" was a triumph for PAUL STEPHENSON (Elmfield, 1926–31; later a BBC producer).

Macduff who "showed great possibilities as an actor" was B. C. SMITH-DORRIEN, (The Head Master's 1925–29) son of the Old Harrovian General who had been in command of the Second Army of the BEF in 1914–15. He himself joined the army and was captured at Tobruk.

THE champion torpids rackets pair, 1930: Derek N. Reed (The Grove 1928–33) (standing) and John H. Pawle (The Grove 1928–34).

Pawle was one of the greatest rackets players the School has produced. He was Public Schools Rackets Champion in 1932 and won both singles and doubles championships in Amateur Rackets. He was Head of The Grove, Captain of School Cricket and a Cambridge University cricket and rackets player.

Torpids are inter-house competitions for boys under 16.

93

THE Philathletic Club in 1930. With no hat, standing on the left, is E. D. B. LABORDE, son of the author of "Harrow School Yesterday and Today." He was killed in 1942. On the extreme right of the second row from the front is SIR TERENCE RATTIGAN, the playwright, author of "The Deep Blue Sea" and of "The Browning Version." Both boys were in The Park.

Next to Rattigan is SIR JOHN HOBSON, Attorney General 1962–64 and a Governor of the School, who died in 1967.

The front row, left to right: SIR JOHN STOW, Governor General of Barbados 1959–66; A. S. LAWRENCE, Captain of Cricket and Athletics 1930, played cricket for Cambridge University, died in 1939; R. D. STEWART-BROWN, Head of School, scholar, double first at Cambridge, QC, in Welsh Guards, died 1963; W. M. WELCH, Captain of Rugby 1929 and of Football 1930, won the Public Schools Eton Fives doubles in 1938, in Rifle Brigade, killed in action at Calais in 1940; D. E. YARROW, doctor, Captain in RAMC.

AN undated photograph showing boys punting on The Park lake, probably in the early 1930s.

Rt Hon Sir Keith Joseph, Bt, CH, MP, Moretons 1931–36, Minister of Housing and Local Government, 1959–61; Minister of State, Board of Trade, 1961–62; Minister of Housing and Local Government and Minister for Welsh Affairs, 1962–64; Secretary of State for Social Services, 1970–74; Secretary of State for Industry 1979–81; Secretary of State for Education and Science 1981–86. In 1987 he was created Baron Joseph of Portsoken in the City of London.

CRICKET matches in progress on the Philathletic Ground in 1931. This field now measures 24 acres, and 24 matches can take place on it simultaneously.

In the background can be seen the Old Schools.

THE Pollok-Morris family, probably taken on Speech Day in 1937.

A reasonably distinguished School Rugby XV of 1937, notable not so much for what they achieved on the field as for what they managed in other spheres. Though they won only a third of their matches, they scored more points than their opponents, including trouncing the Old Harrovians by 31–8.

Left to right, back row: D. G. G. DUSSEK, Ponsonby Scholar, Cambridge University and a Sussex County Rugby player, died 1948; K. W. WALKER, Scottish Boys' Golf Champion while still at School, played golf for Scotland 1950; R. A. A. HOLT, Captain of Cricket and Football 1938, Cambridge University Rackets player, Amateur Rackets Doubles Champion 1949, Chairman of School Governors 1971–80; R. H. S. SILVER, a promising prizewinner in the Royal Navy, killed in action 1943; A. C. PARSONS, Rothschild Scholar, Exhibitioner of Trinity, Cambridge; H. A. VERNEY, Scholar of Oriel, Oxford; G. A. CHURCHER, Balliol, Oxford.

Second row: P. G. B. ALLEN, Captain of Rugby 1938 and of Football 1939, Rothschild Scholar and at Clare, Cambridge; W. S. P. LITHGOW, Christ Church, Oxford, Lt Col in command of the 10th Hussars, and manager of the British Equestrian Three-day-Event Team 1965–76; R. G. SMITH CUNINGHAME, (Captain of the XV) Major in the Black Watch, awarded the Military Cross in 1944, died 1965; D. C. RISSIK, Head of School 1937, Rothschild Scholar 1938, Christ Church, Oxford, author; A. W. LESLIE, Cambridge University, Major in Black Watch, Military Cross in 1945, died 1979.

Front row: W. C. H. GRAY, Captain of the Scottish Boys' Golf Team, 1938, Captain in Royal Artillery, died 1981; W. F. B. POLLOK-MORRIS, Captain of Running 1939–40, Captain in Royal Artillery, Oxford University, Administrator of Ascension Island 1965, died 1976; R. G. TRAILL, Major in Rifle Brigade, Member of Lloyd's.

T HE old gymnasium in the
1930s.

F OUR gymnasts in artistic
pose, *c.* 1938.
Photo: J. S. Armstrong album.

THE Harrow XI taking the field at Lord's *c.* 1938.
Photo: J. S. Armstrong album.

THE Eleven leaving Lord's *c.* 1938.
Photo: J. S. Armstrong album.

THE Butler Museum from the Terrace on Speech Day *c.* 1938.
Photo: J. S. Armstrong album

BOYS in the chemistry labora-
tory before the last war.
Photo: J. S. Armstrong album.

BOYS in the workshops, 1930.
Photo donated by Mr White.

AN exciting moment in a
cycle race, *c.* 1938.
Photo: J. S. Armstrong album.

THE pole vault *c.* 1938 with a ring of boys in straw hats.
Photo: J. S. Armstrong album.

THE pole vault *c.* 1938. The master wearing plus-fours and the boys wearing their straw hats to watch athletics give a period flavour to this action shot. The master was Major B. F. Housden OBE, MC, TD, international pole vaulter and coach.

Photo: Sport and General Press Agency.

A typical "leaver" portrait of the 1930s: D. P. Kelly (Rendalls 1936–39); an American citizen, he died on active service in the Canadian Air Force in 1943.

Photo: J. S. Armstrong album.

THE heavyweight boxer, Jack Petersen, training at The King's Head in the 1930s. He turned professional in 1932 and won the British Light Heavyweight Championship and the British Heavyweight Championship, the only British boxer to have done this in successive fights.

In 1933 he lost his title to Len Harvey but regained it six months later; in 1936 he lost his heavyweight title to Ben Foord. He retired in 1937 with eye trouble.

THE Grove House group in 1939: Mr L. W. Henry is the Housemaster. On the extreme right hand of the second row from the rear is a youthful and bespectacled John Mortimer (J. C. Mortimer, CBE, QC, the playwright; The Grove 1937–40).

SERVICE in progress in Chapel, before the last war.

B. C. BURTON, Custos 1946–68, carving names on one of the house boards. The task is undertaken by each successive holder of the post, using the same mallet as used by Mr Titchener in Churchill's time.

This particular board was for Elmfield, in 1949.

THE Masters in 1951. In the front row on extreme left is a debonair MR A. R. D. WATKINS, Housemaster of Elmfield 1948–58 and the producer of many successful Shakespearean plays; fourth from left is MR J. W. GREENSTOCK, Housemaster of Newlands, 1946–61, whose son became Housemaster in the same House in 1985; eighth from the left is the Head Master, MR R. W. MOORE, who died in office in 1963; behind him is MR S. G. PATTERSON, (1944–82; Housemaster at The Grove 1958–73 and Bursar 1976–80); bearded on the extreme right is MR H. L. HARRIS, Head of English 1948–66 and co-founder of the O.H. Players with His Honour Judge L. J. Verney; holding his top hat on the left is MR B. C. BURTON, Custos 1946–68: next but one to him is MR C. D. LABORDE, Housemaster of The Park, 1960–74, and a stalwart supporter of Harrow football; and second from the right in the centre row is MR M. S. WARMAN, Second Master 1972–79.

THE School Squash VI in 1948. The Captain, David Hodgson (seated centre), was Squash Rackets Champion of South Africa in 1953, D. W. Taylor (standing centre) and T. A. McE. Pigott (seated right) won the Public Schools Rackets Championship in 1948.

R. J. McAlpine (standing right) played Squash Rackets for Wales.

MORETONS House Group with its Housemaster, Mr O. G. Bowlby, in 1952. Third from the left, third row from the front, is H.M. King Faisal II of Iraq, who was assassinated 14 July 1958 (see page 107.)

PANDIT Jawaharlal Nehru (Head Master's 1905–7), Prime Minister of India 1947, seen at a dinner given by Old Harrovians in his honour at the House of Commons in 1952. All the Old Harrovians pictured with him were his contemporaries at school. Left to right: Viscount Long of Wraxall, Earl Alexander of Tunis, Mr Nehru, Mr G. C. Rivington (Governor 1939–69 and Chairman 1953–64), and Sir Walter Monckton.

After the dinner, Winston Churchill and Nehru paid tribute to each other, even though Churchill had been largely responsible for putting Nehru in prison from time to time.

Pandit Nehru's portrait now hangs in Speech Room (see page 67).

THE Classical Sixth Form in 1956, the last taken by Mr E. V. C. Plumptre before his retirement. Of the thirteen boys shown, ten went to Oxford and three to Cambridge, eleven of them with awards. Nine had won scholarships or exhibitions on entering the School.

The group includes N. W. Bethell, now Lord Bethell and a Member of the European Parliament (extreme right in front row) and F. E. R. Butler, (wearing bow tie, front row) now Sir Robin Butler, KCB, CVO, Secretary of the Cabinet, Head of the Home Civil Service, and a School Governor (Chairman 1988). Mr Plumptre was himself a scholar of Hertford College, Oxford, and was a Master 1925–57. For most of that time he was also Vaughan Librarian. He died in 1980.

RENDALLS Cricket XI, 1956. On the extreme right of the back row is P. J. Mitchell, who has restored many of the paintings in the School's collection and is a writer of books on Dutch and Flemish art.

On the right in the front row are James Fox, the actor, and M. B. Connell, QC, who became a School Governor in 1983.

THE School Cricket XI in 1956. Back row, second from right: Mr J. D. C. Vargas, Housemaster of the Head Master's House from 1983; next to him, the tallest of the line is F. E. R. Butler (see page 104).

THE Moretons Rugby XV in 1957. The dark shirt is worn by a "lion", a School Rugby XV player. The boys at the back with tassels on their caps are House Rugby Colours.

H.M. KING Faisal of Iraq (Moretons 1949–52), seen with Dr James in July 1956.

MORETONS Masquerade, 1955. This was an innovative revue, produced by J. H. P. Stedall (1951–55), who is to be seen wearing sunglasses in the centre of the picture, and who "stole the show with his characterisations of an unattractive spinster and low actress". The show was given in the Music Schools and was supervised by Mr Roger Ellis (Master, 1952–67 and Governor from 1987).

HER Majesty Queen Elizabeth II with the Head Master Dr James, passing through the Guard of Honour outside Druries in 1957. Behind them the Duke of Edinburgh is walking beside the Chairman of the Governors, Mr G. C. Rivington.

T HE Queen on the Chapel steps, 1957.

H .M. The Queen under the lych gate at St. Mary's Church with Dr James in 1957.

T HE Queen learns about the Harrow football, 1957 from Mr C. D. Laborde. On the right is the Head Master. The ball, neither round nor oval, is used in Harrow's unique game.

THE Prime Minister, Winston Churchill, arrives for Songs c. 1960. He attended regularly from 1940–1961.
Photo: Keystone Press Agency.

THE School Chess Team 1962–63. (Left to right, rear): J. A. Tobert; G. P. Gretton Watson. (Front): M. T. Tobert; A. P. Nock (Capt); A. C. H. Durham.

110

SOME of the Corps Officers and NCOs in 1960. The Masters in the front row are (left to right): Lt J. A. Strover (1958–70); Lt A. T. Davis (1957–66), Capt M. W. Pailthorpe (1957–): Capt J. M. Rae (1955–66); Lt Cdr G. R. McConnell (1932–68); Maj B. E. D. Cooper (1946–60); Capt A. A. Bishop (1955–); F/O K. W. Wilkes (1953–61); Capt D. P. K. Gaunt (1957–61 and 1972–); Lt J. Jeremy (1957–); and Lt J. C. K. Ingram (1959–).

FOUNDER'S Day 1963; some of those playing Harrow Football for the School or for the Old Harrovians include: (left to right) His Honour Judge L. J. Verney, TD, DL, (in white) (1938–43; Governor 1972–87); P. M. Beckwith (1958-63, Captain of Harrow Football 1963); Dr R. L. James, Head Master 1953–71) and Mr J. F. Leaf (Senior Master 1983–88).

CALLING "Bill" (the School roll-call) in 1964. The boys pass the Head Master, who calls out their names in order and they answer "Here, Sir!" whilst removing their straw hats.
Photo: Keystone Press Agency..

THE Harmony Choir of 1964. The masters to be seen in the second row are (left to right) Mr J. F. Leaf (Master 1951–88, Housemaster of Druries 1968–79, and Senior Master 1983–88); Mr G. J. Higgins (Music Master 1951–67); Rev M. L. Hughes (Chaplain 1961–73); Mr J. P. Lemmon (Master from 1957, Head of English from 1966); Mr R. W. Ellis CBE, (Master 1952–67, Housemaster at The Head Master's 1961–67 and a School Governor from 1987); and Mr S. P. T. Houldsworth (Master 1952–64).

THE Farm Committee in the 1960s, with Mr G. R. D. Parrott, assistant master 1957–80, and farm manager. He died in 1984. The school farm is on the Watford Road; boys help with attending to the 60 cows, including early morning milking. It also contains a hyperbaric oxygen therapy centre for use by multiple sclerosis patients.

AN undated photograph showing the cadets having fire-fighting practice. There appears to be a press photographer on the right getting more than he expected.
Photo: Central Press Photos.

BOYS leaving Chapel after a memorial service on the death of Sir Winston Churchill, January 1965.
Photo: Sport & General Press Agency.

TALKING to her racehorse trainer, whose son was playing on that day, Queen Elizabeth, the Queen Mother, at Lord's in 1968. Eton are batting and have scored 56 for 2, but the boy on the coach seems to have found someone more attractive in the crowd.

The two batsmen at the crease put on 126 for the third wicket, one of them scoring a century, but Harrow won by 7 wickets. The Harrow captain, Indrajit Coomaraswamy, concluded five years in the XI by taking 12 wickets for 92 in the match.

The match was the first to be played at the end of term.
Photo: Sport & General Press Agency.

A graceful arabesque performed by P. J. E. Needham (Bradbys 1965–70), wicket-keeper and Captain of the School Cricket XI, as he tries to run out A. E. Martin-Smith of Eton at Lord's in 1969.

Photo: Sport & General Press Agency.

THE Head Master's House Group in 1968 (Dr R. L. James). Mr G. R. R. Treasure is present as Housemaster at the Head Master's. He later became Housemaster at The Grove and retired from this post in 1988.

MARK Thatcher (Bradbys 1967–71) (right) and J. A. N. Prenn (The Head Master's 1966–71), winners of the Public Schools' Rackets Championship 1971, seen with the rackets professional, Roger Crosby.

Prenn went on to become World Rackets Champion, 1981–84.

ELMFIELD House Group in 1972. Housemaster: Mr M. W. Pailthorpe (Second Master 1983–88, and Housemaster of Elmfield 1971–83).

THE Queen planting a tree by Druries during her visit in 1971.

THE Queen talks to a member of the Corps in parachuting garb during her visit in 1971.

THE Queen and Dr James on the Terrace in 1971. Lord McCorquodale KCVO (in spectacles) accompanies them as Chairman of the Governors.

OVERLEAF:
AN aerial view of the School in 1970 showing the Physics Schools in course of construction. Peel House, the Shepherd Churchill Dining Hall and the sports hall, incorporating the new indoor Ducker, have not yet been built.
Photo: Harrow Observer.

The photographs on this and the following pages were taken between 1983 and 1988, and reflect some aspects of Harrow School in the present day.

CONVERSATION piece under the School Arms on the School Yard gates.

A. K. C. Green, Head of West Acre, amid a sea of hats.

BOYS being served in The Hill restaurant, the School's second line of defence for the insatiable.

BUSY young executive: the Head of West Acre on the telephone in his study.

BOYS queuing to see senior members of the Philathletic Club for minor offences. A knuckle-biting time for some: others have clearer consciences.

THE life-line to home: boys waiting to telephone from the red box that had a preservation order put on it when telephone boxes in Harrow were changed. Gieves, the School tailors, is in the background, with its former lettering, and on the left can be seen the white porch of Moretons.

DISCIPLINARY enquiries in the Philathletic Room. On the walls are team photographs from the middle years of the nineteenth century.

BOYS in the House having their appearance checked by senior boys.

THE School Football XI in 1987, outside the Vaughan Library, in the poses adopted for photographs a hundred years earlier (see page 23).

HARROW Football in action: played with an oddly-shaped ball, it has its own set of rules and an umpire. The "goal posts" (bases) have no crossbars. The Old Harrovians are in white, the School in striped shirts. As no other school plays the game, matches are played between houses or against teams of Old Boys.

MR. B. J. M. Robinson with the Omega timing device in the new 25-metre indoor swimming pool, opened in 1985.

CONVERSATION piece: Mr C. D. Sumner, who retired in 1987, talks to two boys at the top of West Street. The Old House and the School Bookshop are in the background.

THE Head Master, Mr Ian Beer, introduces The Queen to members of the catering staff or her third visit to the school, in 1986; in the centre, Mr M. Egan, Dining Hall Supervisor.

THE scene in Chapel during the Confirmation Service, 1987 (see page 101).

THERE are many sides to the School's musical life: here a jazz group rehearses in West Acre for a concert.

THE War Memorial steps.
BELOW.

AERIAL view of the School showing the Shepherd Churchill Dining Hall which won a Civic Trust award for its architect, Dennis Lennon.
Both photographs by Lichfield.

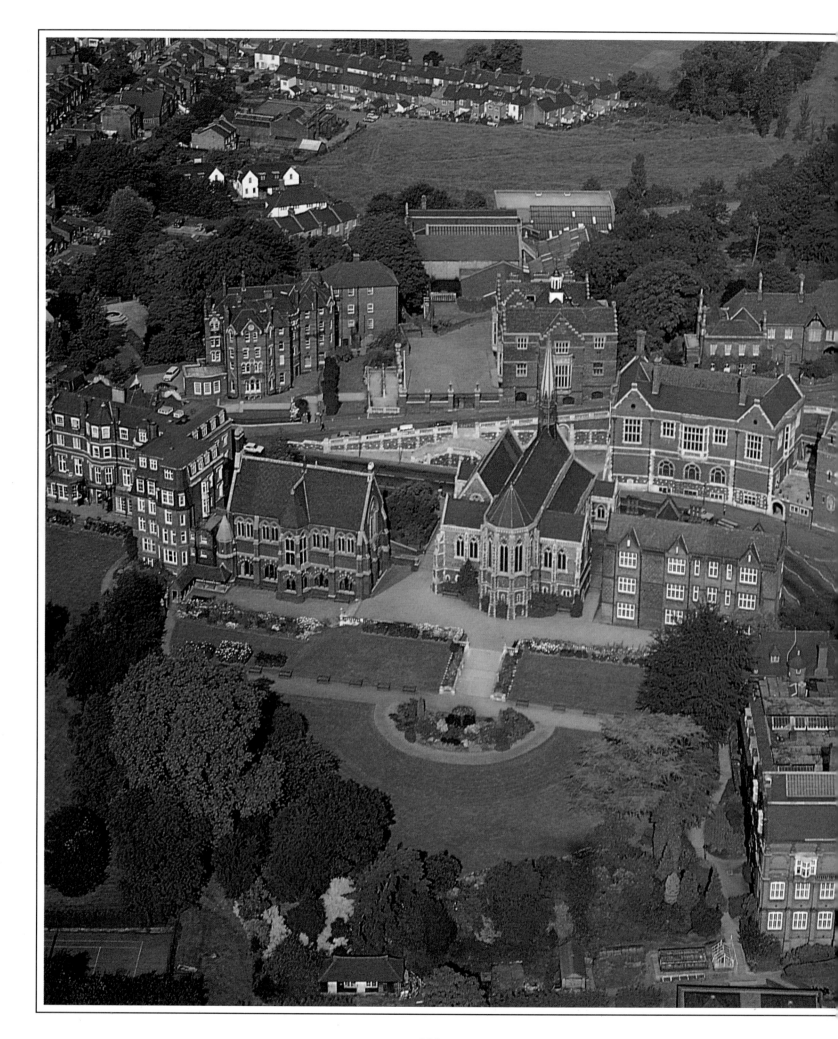

A comprehensive view of the main School buildings, seen from the east. In the centre foreground, can be seen the Museum Schools, designed by Basil Champneys in 1886 to mark the retirement of the Head Master, Dr H. M. Butler. These included not only science laboratories but the School's first museum on the top floor, reached by an external staircase: it is now the Butler Careers Centre.

On the left are the Terrace Gardens, behind which can be seen The Head Master's House, Vaughan Library, Chapel and New Schools. Above them, on the left, Druries stands on guard beside the School Yard and the Old Schools, with the Rackets Courts just visible beyond the yard. Surrounded by trees and the green of Church Fields are St Mary's Church and its vicarage. Between them and the Chapel are the twin gables of the War Memorial, designed by Sir Herbert Baker and completed in 1926, and William Burges's semi-circular Speech Room of 1877.

Partly out of the picture on the right is The Grove, rebuilt after a fire in 1833 and blessed with extensive grounds and ancient woodlands. Below that, a complex of buildings includes the Art Schools (1896 and 1913) and another School House, Rendalls (designed, like the New Schools, by Frederick Barnes).

What is clear from this picture is the way that each architect, at differing periods of the School's history, has designed buildings of distinction that complement each other to form a satisfying whole, by the sympathetic use of suitable materials and building styles.

Photograph by Lichfield.

THE School seen from the nine-hole golf course.

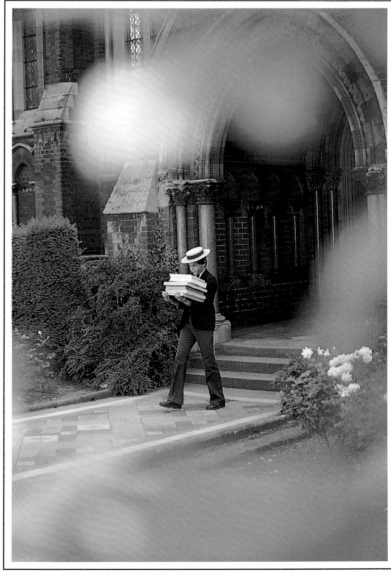

A keen student leaving the Vaughan Library.
Both photographs by Lichfield.

132

SOME of the Governors in 1983, with the Head Master.

Back Row, left to right: Nicholas Owen, Evelyn de Rothschild, Sir Richard Baker Wilbraham, Bt, Hugh Woodcock, Ian Beer, (Head Master), Lt.Gen. Sir John Akehurst, Robson Fisher, Dr Michael Edwards, John Hopkins.

Front Row, left to right: Roger Boissier, Judge Lawrence J. Verney, Sir Peter Green, John Gilbart-Smith, (Clerk to the Governors), Rt Rev Michael Mann, (Chairman), Lady Mary Soames, Dr Michael Grace, Geoffrey Simmonds, Anthony Beresford.

THE Prime Minister, Mrs Thatcher, greeted by the Monitors on her arrival for Churchill Songs, November 1983. She is shaking hand with P. P. Balcombe (Bradbys 1978–83).

THE Masters, 1983. In the front row, left to right are: Messrs Jeremy, Pailthorpe, Treasure, Balme, Venables, Beer (the Head Master), Leaf, Sumner, Bishop, Lemmon and Fothergill.

Behind them stand Messrs Ingram, Shaw, Parsonson, Beckett, Sankey and Bagnall, Sir Allan Outram, Bt, and Messrs Parry, Etheridge and Drakeford.

AN informal group of four of the more senior masters in 1983: (left to right): Mr D. J. Parry (Housemaster of West Acre from 1977); Sir A. J. Outram, Bt (Housemaster of Druries from 1979); Mr M. W. Pailthorpe (Housemaster of Elmfield 1971–83 and Second Master 1983–88), and Mr J. F. Leaf (Housemaster of Druries 1968–79 and Senior Master 1983–88).

MR. M. T. N. Liddiard, OBE, the School Bursar.

H.M. King Hussein of the Hashemites and Queen Noor attending Churchill Songs in December, 1984.
Since Sir Winston's death, these annual concerts of School Songs have been named in his memory. A member of his family usually attends and a prominent visitor makes a speech.

THE Head Master, Mr I. D. S. Beer, greets Her Majesty, Queen Elizabeth, the Queen Mother, when she arrives in November 1985 to attend a service to commemorate Lord Shaftesbury, the Old Harrovian philanthropist. Next to the Queen Mother is the Rt Rev Michael Mann (Moretons 1938–42) Dean of Windsor, Chairman of the Governors 1980–88. Mrs Beer restrains the eager presenter of a posy.

HER Majesty the Queen is saluted by a Guard of Honour on her arrival in November 1986 to lay the foundation stone of the new Craft, Design and Technology Centre, now known as The Churchill Schools. The building was officially opened in 1988 by the Master of Churchill College, Cambridge, (see page 157).

THE Queen attends Churchill Songs November 24, 1986: the scene in Speech Room. Mr P. A. Cartledge conducts the orchestra.

AT the opening of the Sixth Form Club in January 1983, Baroness Soames, daughter of Sir Winston Churchill, unveils the plaque containing a quotation from her father. She is greeted by Mr Geoffrey Simmonds, one of the School Governors and a prime mover in the efforts to raise money in the USA to start this Club, in which members of the Sixth Form may relax from their labours.

Mr Simmonds was at Moretons 1942–47, and while there won the Public Schools Rackets Championship with R. F. K. C. Treherne-Thomas in 1947. He became a Governor in 1975.

MR B. M. S. Hoban (Head Master 1971–81) talks to A. E. J. Bagnall (The Knoll 1979–84), centre, and Daniel Poser (Newlands 1980–84), left, on the same occasion.

CLIFF Richard entertaining the School in Speech Room.

THE cast of "Henry V" in 1984. The production of a Shakespearean play usually occurs in the early part of the Summer Term, a tradition started by Mr A. R. D. Watkins and maintained by Mr J. P. Lemmon.

MONITORS preparing for "Bill" on Speech Day, seen leaving the Fourth Form Room, in 1987. Those visible are, from the top, A. R. Banks, V. A. Umar, T. W. Falcon, M. A. Cook, S. S. Aulak, S. M. Bullivant and M. D. Reynolds.

SEEN from a Druries' window, boys file past the Head Master for the roll-call on Speech Day, known as "Bill".

"BILL" on Speech Day 1986: parents and relatives throng the School yard to watch the ancient ceremony.

BOYS file past the Head Master, and the Head of the School, and answer their names in order.

ROLL Call ("Bill") on Speech Day 1987: boys wearing traditional headgear and carnations.

THE colourful scene in Speech Room on Speech Day 1987: prize giving is in progress. The Second Master (with a red hood) hands books to the Head Master to present to Marigold McVoy. Daughters of masters are now admitted to the Sixth Form.

SPEECH Day gives a chance to show off fancy home-made waistcoats: on the left, one is made from matchsticks and another appears to be a hearthrug.

A fine united-nations waistcoat from T. M. J. Mansur, The Park, 1982.

WAISTCOATS can be most ingenious, being made from newspapers...

...or a bright scarf...

...or from pearl buttons. He carries a flower on his walking stick.

LUNCH on Speech Day with champers on the boot.

...and after it all, a chance to rest.

THE Head Master, Mr I. D. S. Beer, at the head of the Corps, in May, 1983.

THE Head Master in unfamiliar garb, with the inspecting officer, Commodore A. Casdagli. Between them is Major J. R. Beckett, Commanding Officer of the Corps and Housemaster of Elmfield since 1983, shortly after this picture was taken. On the extreme left in the background is Major H. C. Blosse Lynch (Elmfield 1947–51) of the Irish Guards.

THE cadets practise para-scending.

THE Rendalls Assault Course Competition winners in 1983: the course is a severe test of stamina, determination – and the School Laundry.

THE Second World War memorial, remembering 344 Old Harrovians who died 1939–45 and in other conflicts afterwards.

The shrine at the entrance to the War Memorial commemorates the 644 Old Boys who died in the First World War, 1914–1918.

FLY-on-the wall technique from a wasp? A party of eastern visitors, observing a boy on the climbing wall on the outside of the new Sports Centre, wondered if it was some form of fiendish punishment for bad behaviour.

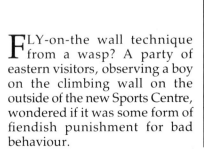

Mr D. R. Elleray, Head of Geography, and a professional referee, with the School Association Football XI 1987, and reserves.

Mr P. J. Higgins with the School Clay Pigeon Shooting team, 1987.

MR R. M. Uttley, former Captain of the England Rugby XV and England's Rugby Coach in 1988, with the School Senior Basketball Team, 1987.

Mr J. L. Ing is at the back on the right.

THE School Karate team in 1985 looking remarkably angelic; the master in charge is Mr R. D. Burden (third from left, rear row).

THE School Fencing Team, 1983. The master in charge is Dr J. E. C. Holland. The sole rose among the thorns is Juliet Leaf (Elmfield 1982–84).

MR P. G. Dunbar with the winning under-16 Public Schools Fives Champions of 1983, C. Stilianopoulos and T. F. Dajani, both of Newlands.

PAUL Balcombe (Bradbys 1978–83) collects the ball from the scrum.

A nine-hole golf course has been in use in the School grounds for over ten years. Here N. J. Southward (Moretons 1980–84) demonstrates his swing.

M ANY of the boys' houses are being refurbished, and a new building has been erected for The Knoll. Boys are seen here at work in one of the new study rooms.

M R M. E. Smith teaching Economics to the Sixth Form with the aid of an overhead projector.

The establishment of a Resources Centre has made the provision of visual aids much more efficient.

Economics teaching started in the 1930s under Mr E. D. Laborde.

THE Harrow Straw, showing its wide brim and narrow crown. It was originally worn only for cricket matches.

AGAINST a background of the carved names of some of their predecessors in the Fourth Form Room, senior boys model a selection of the colourful blazers worn to indicate their status in the House: at the rear, Moretons, Druries and Newlands; in front, The Grove, Sixth Form Coat, West Acre and Elmfield.

D RURIES, one of the oldest of the eleven School Houses: it was named after previous Housemasters of the Drury family.

M R. S. G. Wilkinson, Custos from 1968 to 1983.

T HE Marmots Club, 1983, with Mr. M. C. Greenstock and Mr. D. J. Farrant. They are the group interested in mountain climbing; they are here seen outside the back of Druries, beside Dove House.

154

THE Park Cock House Rugby Seven 1984/5, with the house in the background. The captain, second from right in the front row, was B. D. Rugge-Price.

BRADBYS Cock House football team 1983, seen in their distinctive colours on the flat roof of their House before renovation removed this convenient setting.

JUSTINE Beckett, daughter of the Housemaster of Elmfield, seen in the House Group in 1986, before she joined the School. Also in the picture are Richard Pyman, who captained the School Cricket XI, and Robert Portal, one of the stars of "Henry V" in 1984 (see page 139).

MR E. A. Escritt, Head of Resources, re-enacts the School party's visit to Jordan in April 1988 with two of the boys who went on the expedition.

156

SPEECH Day, 1988: in glorious sunshine, parents and friends watch "Bill" in the School Yard, as the Head Master, Mr I. D. S. Beer, calls the names and the Head of School, C. O. Bridgeman, assists. Bridgeman is the seventh Harrovian in direct line of descent from the first Earl of Bradford, who was at the School in 1770.

PROFESSOR Sir Hermann Bondi, KCB, FRS, Master of Churchill College, Cambridge, opening the new Churchill Schools in April 1988. Named after Sir Winston, these include facilities for craft, design, technology, geography and computer studies. On the left is Mr R. M. L. Bracey, Director of Computing.

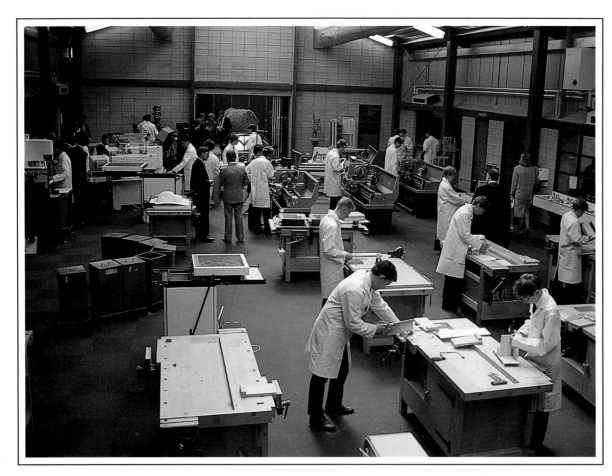

A general view of the new craft workshop with its carpeted floor and white-coated operatives.

THE Lady Soames, DBE, daughter of Sir Winston Churchill and one of the School Governors, with her nephew, Mr Winston Churchill, MP, and his wife, inspecting the computers in the new Churchill Schools in April 1988.

IN the design studio of the new Churchill Schools, a student considers the options available with the "paintbox" facility on his computer.

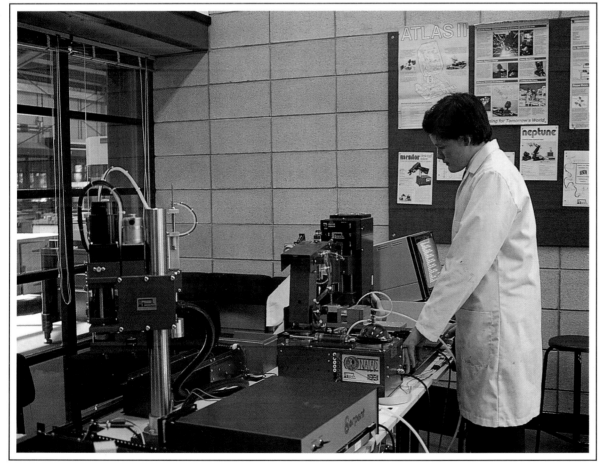

IN the Churchill Schools, a boy ponders a problem in robotics. A conveyor-belt operation, designed by boys in the Remove, was demonstrated on Speech Day. In the Design Studio, other boys have tackled such practical problems as designing a hand cart for manoeuvring large bales of hay on a farm or how to carry hockey sticks on a bicycle.

A window in the Fitch Room in the War Memorial, showing John Lyon, the Founder of the School, consulting the architect's plans for the building of his new school. He intended it as a free grammar school for local boys, to enable them to rise to the highest positions of authority in the country. By the fortunate inclusion in his Statutes of a clause allowing the Head Master to admit fee-payers, his wildest dreams must have come true: eight boys, including Pandit Nehru of India, have become Prime Ministers. From his humble act of charity to his native town has grown a school of world renown, that has produced archbishops, a cardinal, great statesmen, famed military leaders, thinkers, scientists and writers, as well as sportsmen, artists – and photographers.

John Lyon would surely have been proud of the Harrow School of today, with its exciting developments to meet the challenges of the twenty-first century, and he would certainly have approved the motto adopted in 1805:

Stet Fortuna Domus.